MW00511360

TO: _____

FROM: _____

FOREWORD

When we met Dave, we immediately knew he was probably too cool for us. He's tattooed; he's hip; he has that amazing Australian accent. He came barreling into our organization filled with great questions and fresh ideas. None of that surprised us. But what did catch us a bit off guard was his multi-faceted talent. Not only was he exceptional at his media production job, but we discovered he was particularly adept at all things social media. Then we were introduced to his photography ... Wow!

Over dinner one evening Dave and Meg allowed us to peek into their world. Dave shared the powerful story of his childhood, and how God leveraged and redeemed what could have easily derailed his life. We were inspired, challenged, and in complete awe of God's ability to heal what has been shattered and broken.

Sometimes it's those very painful things that deepen faith and deliver a fresh lens through which to view life. Dave began using his photographs to teach biblical truths to his daughters in a way that was creative and memorable. He started sharing them via Instagram, and his following exploded. We are thrilled that he is now taking those very same devotionals and photographs and making them available in this beautiful book.

So, Dave, thank you for not being too cool for these middle-aged Americans. We're extraordinarily proud of you, and grateful God allowed our paths to cross.

Sandra and Andy Stanley

SHOUT OUTS!

From the moment I met Aussie Dave, his words and devotions have been a source of encouragement for me. He has such unique and creative insights into biblical stories and symbols, and he shares them passionately because he wants to give people hope and understanding. I know his words and his amazing photography will connect with everyone who reads this book as much as they have with me.

Lauren Daigle, Grammy nominated singer/songwriter, Dove Award and Billboard Award winner

I love that in a visual age filled with new wonder, authors like Dave Adamson are finding fresh ways to tell timeless stories like this!

Jon Acuff, New York Times Bestselling Author and Speaker

By pairing his stunning photography with biblical truths, Dave Adamson gives us the chance to see, believe, and hear. Throughout these pages of *Chasing the Light* we have the opportunity to quiet ourselves in order to hear God's whisper.

Rebekah Lyons, Author of Freefall to Fly

As an artist and photographer I am keenly aware of how creativity can bring new insight and understanding, which is exactly what Dave Adamson does with this book. He connects beautiful, modern photography with the rich, ancient story of the Bible to bring fresh, deeper understanding. It's more than a devotional and more than a photography book — it's a creative insight into faith.

Jeremy Cowart, Photographer and Founder of The Purpose Hotel.

SHOUT OUTS!

Dave Adamson is inspiring a whole generation through the combination of photos and writing, and continues to connect the dots of hope and faith through this powerful devotional. *Chasing the Light* should be on your desk, coffee table, and nightstand.
Brad Lomenick, *Author of* H3 Leadership *and* The Catalyst Leader.

If our faith is only conceived of in words, we are ignoring what is constantly before us from morning to night, and even when we dream: images filled with emotions, insight, and power. Dave Adamson's wonderful devotional taps into some brilliant images from nature and the human drama, and reminds us that "The heavens are telling of the glory of the Lord."
Peter Enns, *Author of* The Bible Tells Me So *and* The Sin of Certainty.

So many Christians know that Scripture is rich with meaning and insight, and yet many of us miss that richness when we read it. Dave Adamson never does. He has a unique gift of lifting well-known and less-well-known Scripture texts, offering clear insight, and setting it all against a backdrop of stunning photography. I love Dave's art and insight, and I know you will too.
Carey Nieuwhof, *Lead Pastor, Connexus Church.*

Chasing the Light will help illuminate your faith. It's what my friend Dave Adamson does for so many people through his art, teaching, and most importantly, friendship. Think of these devotions as 90 lighthouses shining the path to the One who knows and loves you best. And as you live out these messages of hope, the Light will shine even brighter through you. That's how the Kingdom works. After all, "you are the light of the world . . ."
Jeff Henderson, *Lead Pastor, Gwinnett Church.*

SHOUT OUTS!

If the cliché that "a picture is worth a thousand words" is true, this book says a lot. Dave has a knack for beautiful snaps, but the wisdom that he couples with his pictures makes this book worth your time and attention. Not only will his work give you lift, but it will also help you learn to find God in the smallest of moments. And that's worth a thousand pictures. Thank you, Dave!

Clay Scroggins, *Lead Pastor, North Point Community Church.*

Dave Adamson is one of the most unique and gifted men I know. I love this man and his gifts for so many reasons. He loves God, as you can see in the deep and rich insights he brings from God's Word, especially from the original languages. He has a keen eye for God's glorious creation, which he captures in stunning and magnificent photographs. But most of all, I love his love for his beautiful wife and daughters. He inspires me daily. Study his photographs. Ponder his insights. You will be changed. Daily.

John Woodall, *Director of (7), North Point Ministries.*

There are lots of great pastors in the world whose hearts are inclined to shepherd and encourage followers of Jesus Christ. There are a lot of people who have a solid grasp of what the Bible says and a knack for communicating that to others. And then there are all the skilled photographers, those folks who have the artistic and technical skills to capture compelling images. But I know of only one man, Dave Adamson, who possesses all three gifts. It's our great good fortune that he's published his first book, *Chasing the Light.* Don't miss this chance to have your faith strengthened by Dave's insight into the Scriptures and your heart inspired by the beauty he's captured.

John Hambrick, *Author of* Move Toward the Mess.

SHOUT OUTS!

God speaks to the heart and the mind. In his stunning book, Dave Adamson does the same. The images alone inspire and uplift. The words alone instruct and engage. Together they create a unique whole that brings divine wisdom and hope into our lives. I love this book, and will share it with friends and students for years to come.

Rabbi Evan Moffic, *Author,* What Every Christian Needs to Know About the Jewishness of Jesus

There is something incredible about God's creation and His words that change our view of the world. Dave Adamson has done a brilliant job of combining these two art forms to create this amazing work.

Tyler Reagin, *Executive Director of Catalyst.*

SHOUT OUTS!

This book is a great way to learn a lot about God and Jesus. I know this because my dad teaches me about the Bible by showing me one of his photos and then teaching me how it's like a story in the Bible. The way my dad uses photos has helped me learn about God and understand the Bible better. I think he's the best dad in the whole world!

Jordyn Adamson, 12

I'm so happy and proud that my dad was able to take his amazing photos and turn it into a book. I think it's awesome that his love for God and photography can be put into something you can read and hold. He's an awesome dad.

Ella Adamson, 13

My dad teaches my sisters and me about the Bible all the time. He knows so much about it. He's also really good at photography, so he has put these two talents together to help us understand the Bible. He started out on Instagram, and from there he's been on multiple podcasts and websites, and even told his story at many churches. Now he's putting out his very first book! Well done, Dad, I'm proud of you.

Chelsea Adamson, 16

ISBN: 978-0997636802
Printed in China

You know how it is when you get a new book and flip to the dedication page hoping to see your name . . . well, I honestly couldn't list you all by name, sorry. But I do want to thank everyone who encouraged and — those who nagged — me to create this book. You know who you are. I also want to thank everyone who reads my posts on www.instagram.com/aussiedave and those who have traveled with me on the journey of faith — you know who you are too.

To my three girls, Chelsea, Ella and Jordyn . . .
You're the reason I write these devotions. Without you . . . I would probably have finished this book 10 years ago. Thanks for distracting me with fun, laughs, funny Vines, and Nerf wars.

And to my wife, Meg, you make my world turn.

BE STILL AND KN

THAT I AM GOD

PSALM 46:10

LET IT GO

Just about every Christian I know struggles with anxiety. For me, anxiety can swirl around in my head like a storm cloud. Being still before God and not stressing is often easier said than done. Instead, I try to take control of situations that are actually out of my control. The verb "be still" in Hebrew is the word *raphah*, which literally means "to let go" or "to surrender." Being still before God means letting go of our need to control the world around us. When we do this, the light of God can break through the storm clouds overhead.

Are you worried and anxious today? Take a moment to still yourself before God right now ... and surrender your desire to control the situation to Him.

He says, "Be still, and know that I am God; I will be exalted among the nations, I will be exalted in the earth."
Psalm 46:10

HEARING FROM GOD

When you walk along a beach and go under a pier, one of the first things you notice is the sound difference. Waves and voices bounce and echo off pylons, adding reverb and volume, so everything sounds louder and clearer. Sometimes in order to hear something better, you need to put yourself in the best place to hear clearly. It's the same with God. If you want to hear from God, you need to:

1. WITHDRAW. You need to get away from the "noise" in your life.
2. WAIT. In "Psalm 62:1 (NLT) we read "I wait quietly before God" . . . you need to be patient.
3. READ the Word of God. As Rick Warren says: "Sometimes you need to stop waiting for a voice and start looking for a verse" in order to hear from God.

Do you want to hear from God today?

But He said, "On the contrary, blessed are those who hear the word of God and observe it."
Luke 11:28, *NASB*

4

HE RENEWS
MY STRENGTH.
HE GUIDES
ME ALONG
RIGHT PATHS

PSALM 23:3

WALKING ON STRAIGHT PATHS

The road we walk on in life is full of ups and downs. Sometimes you're struggling uphill, other times you're out of control, careening downhill. But in Psalm 23 we read that God leads us on "straight" or "righteous" paths . . . so what does that mean when your life feels more like a roller coaster?

In the desert, shepherds can't lead their sheep straight up or down a hill or the sheep will stagger out of control, fall down, and hurt themselves. Instead, shepherds use their voice to lead their sheep to narrow paths that wind around the hill and allow the sheep to travel up and down unharmed. Likewise, if we want to survive life's ups and downs, we need God to guide us to the straight paths He has prepared. But we can't be guided if we're distracted and don't hear His voice.

If your life feels like a twisting roller coaster today, focus on God's voice and let Him guide you to the straight path.

He renews my strength. He guides me along right paths, bringing honor to his name.
Psalm 23:3, NLT

HEAR O ISRAEL:
THE LORD IS
OUR GOD
THE LORD ALONE

DEUTERONOMY 6:4

ARE YOU HEARING GOD?

I know people who feel closest to God when they see a sunrise on the beach, and others when they're worshiping through music. Personally, I feel connected to God when I'm learning something new about Him.

The people of the Bible connected with God through a prayer they recited every morning and night called the *Shema*. The word *shema* means "hear" and comes directly from this verse in Deuteronomy 6. Even today, Jews recite this passage morning and night as a way of drawing close to God and committing themselves to following Him every day.

How do you connect with God and commit yourself to Him every day?

Hear, O Israel: The LORD our God, the LORD is one.
Deuteronomy 6:4

IF YOU ASK ME ANYTHING IN
MY NAME I WILL DO IT

JOHN 14:14

A BOOK OF QUESTIONS

My youngest daughter once asked me where seashells come from. I had no idea, but I was glad she saw me as the place to go for answers. While we often view the Bible in the same way, the ancient Jews viewed it not as a "Book of Answers" for our questions but instead as a "Book of Questions" for our answers. They believed we learn more when we honestly wrestle with a question than when we're just given an answer.

Think about it . . . one of the first things God says to man is a question: "Where are you?" (Genesis 3:9). This is the question of a Father seeking a lost child. The Bible, like this first question, is designed to lead us out of hiding so we can respond to our Father.

What question is God asking of you today?

Ask me for anything in my name, and I will do it!
John 14:14, NLT

10

A SPACIOUS PLACE

Whenever I feel stressed or overwhelmed, I've always found that going to wide open spaces like Bells Beach, Australia, has helped. There are several verses in the Bible that describe this too: "He brought me out into a spacious place" (Psalm 18:19) or "you have set my feet in a spacious place" (Psalm 31:8). In Hebrew, the root word used here, *rachab*, means "wide" or "spacious." But *rachab* also means "to breathe" or "be refreshed," which helps explain why wide spaces relieve stress — they are created to give us room to breathe.

Do you feel stressed today? Is your world caving in? Are you struggling with an issue? Ask God to set your feet in a spacious place (a *rachab*) so you have room to breathe in His Spirit.

He brought me out into a spacious place; he rescued me because he delighted in me.
2 Samuel 22:20

ALL THAT YOU NEED

Whenever I imagined the green pasture of Psalm 23, it always looked something like this. This fits the verse, right? "The LORD is my shepherd, I have all that I need. He lets me rest in green meadows; He leads me beside peaceful streams." It sounds like the sheep never have any trouble. But in a field like this with endless grass and shade . . . a sheep doesn't need a shepherd at all.

"I have all that I need" does not mean "I won't need anything ever again . . . even God!" The promise is that we will have all we NEED, not all that we WANT.

God doesn't always give you the circumstances or people that you WANT. . . . He gives you the circumstances and people that you NEED. Sometimes what we need is to rely on God while we're in the valley of the shadow of death.

Maybe it's time you changed your perspective.

The LORD is my shepherd, I lack nothing. He makes me lie down in green pastures, he leads me beside quiet waters.
Psalm 23:1–2

14

WALK HUMBLY WITH YOUR GOD.

MICAH 6:8

NOTHING MORE, NOTHING LESS

Have you ever been humbled by nature? Have you ever walked through a field of tulips or watched a sunset and been reminded of how incredibly awesome God is and how small you are by comparison? It's humbling. The Hebrew word *ávanah* is what we translate as "humility," but the literal definition of *ávanah* is to occupy your God-given space in the world — not to overestimate yourself or your abilities, and to not underestimate them either.

We live in a world of likes, retweets, followers, fans, and favorites, and it's easy to determine our self-worth based on how many or how few of these we have. Even many of our national leaders model a lifestyle based on belittling people with different views while bragging about themselves.

What if, just for today, you resolved to simply serve others by taking up the space God has given you to occupy? Nothing more, nothing less.

He has shown you, O mortal, what is good. And what does the LORD require of you? To act justly and to love mercy and to walk humbly with your God.
Micah 6:8

WALKING INTIMATELY WITH GOD

Driving into New York City at night, you can see the glow of the neon lights from miles away. It always reminds me of Jesus telling His followers they were "a city on a hilltop that cannot be hidden" (Matthew 5:14). He wanted their faith to "shine out for all to see" (v. 16). But how do you do that?

I believe part of the answer is summed up in the Hebrew word *hasidut*, which means to walk intimately with God and live to serve Him. *Hasidut* means obeying God out of love. *Hasidut* will change the way you behave and how you serve those around you. It's like my friend Andy Stanley says, "Your devotion to God is illustrated, demonstrated, and authenticated by your love for others." This is *hasidut*.

Will the way you treat others today bring glory to God?

You are the light of the world — like a city on a hilltop that cannot be hidden.
Matthew 5:14, NLT

YOU ARE THE LIGHT OF THE WORLD,
LIKE A CITY ON A HILLTOP THAT CANNOT BE HIDDEN.

MATTHEW 5:14

LET YOUR LIGHT SHINE

The Jewish rabbis have a centuries-old expression that the health of someone's eye is an indication of their attitude toward generosity. Someone with a "good eye" (*ayin tovah* in Hebrew) is generous to those in need, while someone with a "bad eye" is stingy. Jesus once told His disciples that if their eyes were "healthy" they would be "filled with light" (Luke 11:34, NLT). His point was that if we look for ways to serve others and have an attitude of generosity, then our lives will be illuminated from the inside out.

Whenever you serve and care for those around you, your faith and good deeds will shine before others and bring glory to God. Imagine what the world would look like if Christians believed this and consciously looked for ways to care for the people around them every day. Could you do it today?

The eye is the lamp of the body. If your eyes are healthy, your whole body will be full of light.
Matthew 6:22

A PURPOSE FOR PAIN

We all cry. We all weep. We all suffer. We all mourn.

While this verse from the book of Revelation offers hope for the future, hope can also be found in the present by knowing that even Jesus cried. When His friend Lazarus died, Jesus wept even though He knew He was about to raise Lazarus back to life (John 11:35). Jesus felt the pain of the people around Him, and so He cried with them.

I'm sure there are people reading these words today who woke up with burdens, pain, loss, and stress. Whatever you're facing today, know that Jesus understands and has a purpose for your pain. As C.S. Lewis said, "hardship often prepares an ordinary person for an extraordinary destiny."

How would you face your struggles today if you believed without a doubt that God was using this hard time to prepare you for something extraordinary?

He will wipe every tear from their eyes. There will be no more death or mourning or crying or pain, for the old order of things has passed away.
Revelation 21:4

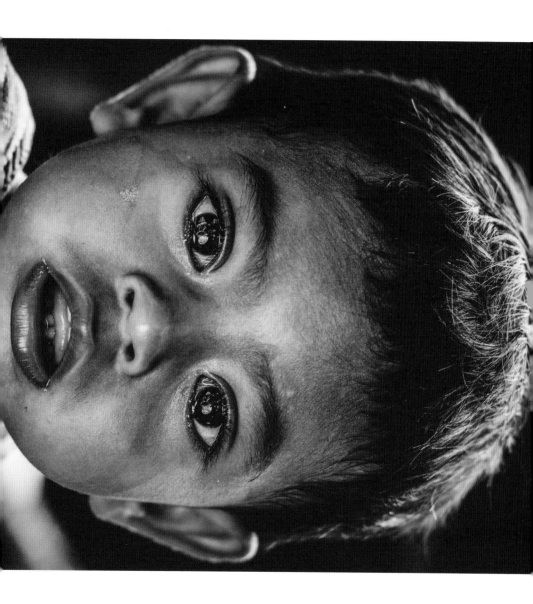

DEFEAT INTO VICTORY

Have you ever noticed that people of a particular culture or place just "know" things that are relevant to them? For example, this old jetty is so well known on the surf coast of Victoria, Australia, that if I showed this photo to a local, they'd know it's the old Clifton Springs pier.

It's the same with the Bible. If I say, "Our Father who art in Heaven," most of you would know the next line, who said it, and in what context. Jesus often expected His audience to have this sort of understanding . . . even when He was on the cross and said, "My God, my God, why have you forsaken me?" It may seem like He was crying out to God, but Jewish believers knew

He was quoting Psalm 22. They knew this is not a psalm of defeat — despite this opening line — but it's actually about victory.

Even on the cross, Jesus wanted people to know that God would be victorious, so He quoted a psalm of hope and resurrection that ends with God being praised as King!

He reveals deep and hidden things; he knows what lies in darkness, and light dwells with him.
Daniel 2:22

TO GOD ALONE

Before he composed any piece of music, Johann Sebastian Bach would pray out loud: "Jesus, help me show your glory," and then write the letters "JJ" on the top of a blank sheet of paper. JJ was short for *Jesu Juva*, which is Latin for "Jesus, help." Once he was finally satisfied with the music he'd written, Bach would write "S.D.G" at the bottom of the page, which stood for *Soli Deo Gloria* — "to God alone the glory."

This is my guitar. As a musician, I love the way Bach directed glory back to God through his music. But I think this is an idea we can all use. Imagine how your faith would change if you started every day and every interaction by saying "*Jesu Juva*," and then made sure to say "To God alone the glory" at the end of every day!

Whether you're facing a day of turmoil or you have a fun day ahead, you need Jesus' help. And at the end of today, regardless of what has happened, God deserves glory for all you've been through.

To our God and Father be glory for ever and ever. Amen.
Philippians 4:20

IN CONTROL OF CHAOS

During Bible times the sea had a negative connotation for the Jewish people. Even today, there aren't many houses or hotels on the Sea of Galilee for this reason. In fact, the Hebrew word for water — *mayim* — comes from the root *mah* or *mem*, meaning "chaos," which makes sense when you consider that the Israelites grew up hearing that a flood wiped out the earth.

So why then does Jesus "insist" that His disciples cross the Sea of Galilee during a storm (Mark 6:45, NLT)? He sent them into the chaos! But then He came to help them by walking on top of the water, showing that He is in total control of ALL chaos.

Are you facing turmoil today? Remember that Jesus is in control of your chaos, and He's calling you to get on top of the chaos with Him. Are you ready to let Jesus take control of your chaos?

They had rowed three or four miles when suddenly they saw Jesus walking on the water toward the boat.
John 6:19, NLT

THEY SAW JESUS WALKING ON THE WATER

JOHN 6:19

THE SOURCE OF LIFE

Just about every major city in the world has a river running through it. In New York it's the Hudson. In London it's the Thames. Paris has the Seine. Melbourne has the Yarra River. These rivers were once vital to the life of the city because they provided a supply line that allowed boats loaded with food and other goods to reach the city. Today these rivers are still a source of life because so many restaurants and hotels are located on their banks.

The ancient Jews called rivers *mayim chayim*, which means "living water," because for a people living in the desert, this water literally provided life. Once, at an annual feast called Sukkot, which celebrated God's provision of living water, Jesus stood and said that anyone who followed Him would have living water streaming out of them. He was saying that His followers would be refreshing and life-giving to everyone they came in contact with.

Will you be a source of life and refreshment to your friends, neighbors, or coworkers today?

But those who drink the water I give will never be thirsty again. It becomes a fresh, bubbling spring within them, giving them eternal life.
John 4:14, NLT

LIGHTING THE WAY

I took this photo early one morning at Point Lonsdale, on the surf coast of Australia. I could only see a few feet ahead of me and needed the pier lights to guide me. I was reminded of the words of Jesus: "he who loves me will be loved by my Father, and I will love him and manifest myself to him" (John 14:21, ESV). This verse came to mind because the Greek word for *manifest* means "to shine" like these pier lights.

What Jesus was saying is that when we love, worship, and praise God, His light shines in us. The Hebrew word for "shine" — *tehillah* — also means "praise." So when we love God, we shine with Jesus AND we praise Jesus all at the same time.

Just as these pier lights directed me through the fog, the presence of Jesus should shine in you today and direct others to God.

Whoever has my commands and keeps them is the one who loves me. The one who loves me will be loved by my Father, and I too will love them and show myself to them.

John 14:21

THE ONE WHO LOVES ME WILL BE LOVED BY MY FATHER, AND I WILL LOVE HIM AND WILL MANIFEST MYSELF TO HIM

JOHN 14:21

ISN'T IT OBVIOUS THAT GOD-TAL

WITHOUT GOD-ACTS

IS OUTRAGEOUS NONSENSE?

JAMES 2:17

DEFINING YOUR FAITH

When I first started following God, I thought faith was an intellectual decision: I knew there was a God, so therefore I had faith. But the Hebrew word for "faith"— *émuwnah* — is less about KNOWING, and more about DOING.

Émuwnah literally means "to take firm action," so to have faith is to act. It's kind of like a staircase; you may intellectually know that the stairs go up to the next level, but until you climb the stairs you won't *experience* the next level. What you do is more important than what you know. Don't just believe in the stairs, climb the stairs.

What do you need to change today to ensure your faith is defined by what you do, instead of what you know?

Isn't it obvious that God-talk without God-acts is outrageous nonsense?
James 2:17, MSG

BRING OUT THE GOD-COLORS

In the time of Jesus, Jerusalem was the crossroads of the world. Empires and kingdoms that wanted to trade in that part of the world had to either go through Jerusalem or spend weeks at sea. It's no coincidence that God placed His people along the main street of the ancient world. He wanted the world to see His followers living out their faith.

I believe God wants the same for us today. As this verse says, He wants us to bring out the God-colors in the world and point people to Him by the way we serve, encourage, and support those around us.

How will you point people to God today?

You're here to be light, bringing out the God-colors in the world.
Matthew 5:14, MSG

TRUSTING THE SHEPHERD

Jesus described Himself as a Good Shepherd who is willing to lay down His life to protect His sheep. While I always understood this idea in theory, I missed the significance because where I come from, sheep are kept safe inside fenced-off paddocks with food and water, so they don't need a shepherd.

But Jesus calls His followers to be out in the world beyond the fence line, where the dangers are real. This is where we are compelled to rely on Jesus and have faith in our Shepherd's promise. We have to trust that He will step in to take care of us in every situation.

Are you staying safe behind the fence? Or are you going out to where Jesus is calling you and where you have to rely on Him?

"I am the good shepherd; I know my own sheep, and they know me — just as the Father knows me and I know the Father — and I lay down my life for the sheep."
John 10:14–15

I AM THE
GOOD SHEPHERD
I KNOW
MY SHEEP
AND THEY
KNOW ME

HERE COMES THE SUN

When a kid named Matthew told the story of Jesus walking on the water (Matthew 14), he said it was during the "fourth watch" that the disciples saw their rabbi strolling on the lake. The fourth watch was from 3 a.m. to 6 a.m. — the final watch going from the darkest part of the night until the sun rose. In fact, some translations say that it was "just before dawn" that Jesus walked on the sea.

During a family vacation, we had a spectacular view of the sunrise over the Gulf of Mexico. My daughter Ella would get up and watch with me each morning, and say, "Here comes the sun!" when the light first appeared over the horizon. When Jesus the Light of the World walked on the water toward His disciples just before dawn, I wonder if they said the same thing.

Be reminded today that when things are darkest, that's when the Light of the World comes.

And in the fourth watch of the night he came to them, walking on the sea.
Matthew 14:25, ESV

BE TRANSFORMED

This tree along the surf coast of Australia is not deformed. Despite a strong trunk, deep roots, and thick branches, this tree is bent over because the strong prevailing winds that blow through the region transformed it from the time it first started to shoot leaves. This tree is strong and healthy, it has just been influenced by the power of the wind.

This tree is a picture of the way we are transformed by the Spirit of God. The Hebrew word for wind is *ruwach*, which also means "Spirit" or "breath" of God. When we choose to let the *ruwach* of God transform and influence

41

us, we will look different — just like these trees — to the people around us. We will stand out.

You are influenced and transformed by something — either the people you spend time with, the choices you make, or the Spirit of God. Your life doesn't get transformed by chance . . . it gets transformed by choice.

Instead, let the Spirit renew your thoughts and attitudes.
Ephesians 4:23, NLT

42

KNOWING YOU'RE DEVOTED

In two different places, two different authors in the Bible write that "the earth will be filled with the knowledge of the LORD, as the waters cover the sea" (Habakkuk 2:14; Isaiah 11:9). Because I interpret the word knowledge as "facts," I used to think this verse meant everyone on earth would know the facts about the existence of God.

But the Hebrew word for "knowledge" in these verses is *yadá*, which means "to know from experience and relationship." So for the ancient Jews, to have "knowledge of God" was to have a life devoted to experiencing Him. By using the word *yadá*, these two verses are saying that one day "the earth will be filled with devotion for the LORD as water covers the sea."

Would people say that about you? Would they say your life is filled with devotion to God?

For the earth will be filled with the knowledge of the glory of the LORD as the waters cover the sea.
Habakkuk 2:14

MAKING A DIFFERENCE

I read a quote once that said "each of us is a unique strand in the intricate web of life and here to make a difference." Do you feel like your faith makes a difference in the lives of the people around you? I once asked a rabbi friend what he recommended for spiritual growth that would make a difference in me and others, and he said to "pray every day, read Scripture every day, and give to charity every day for a balance of knowledge, prayer, and acts of loving-kindness." What a challenge!

Imagine the difference it would make in your community if every Christian you knew valued acts of loving-kindness to our neighbors as much as we value quoting Scripture.

And don't forget to do good and to share with those in need. These are the sacrifices that please God.
Hebrews 13:16, *NLT*

BE CONFIDENT

There's a line in the Bible that I struggled with for years. It reads: "For he gives his sunlight to both the evil and the good, and he sends rain on the just and the unjust alike." (Matthew 5:45, NLT). I often wondered why God would choose to give light and warmth to people who don't acknowledge or love Him. Then I realized that it's because He loves them.

As Christians, I think we get so focused on our love for God that it can be easy to forget about how much HE loves US! The first Jewish believers understood the Bible to be a collection of stories that weren't about how much certain people loved God . . . but about how much God loved them! The sun shines on people because God loves them no matter what. The Bible is not a book about you loving God, but about God loving you.

What would your life look like if you lived with a deep understanding of and confidence in how much God loves you?

But I say to you, Love your enemies and pray for those who persecute you, so that you may be sons of your Father who is in heaven. For he makes his sun rise on the evil and on the good, and sends rain on the just and on the unjust.
Matthew 5:44–45, ESV

REST IN HIS SHADOW

How do you describe God? Western Christians often describe Him as holy, almighty, or simply love, but to a Jewish believer, God is more tangible — you can touch, taste, smell, and experience Him. The book of Psalms describes God as the "shade at your right hand" (Psalm 121:5). The Hebrew word for "shade" is *tsel*, which means "protection."

I grew up in Australia, where summer temperatures soar above 110 degrees Fahrenheit. This sort of heat literally buckles train tracks, but in the shade things are more comfortable. I understood this Hebrew idea of shade being protection.

Today, are you being burned by life? God wants you to know that He is your shade, and whoever "dwells in the shelter of the Most High will rest in the shadow (*tsel*) of the Almighty" (Psalm 91:1).

When you see shade today, be reminded that God is with you.

The LORD watches over you — the LORD is your shade at your right hand.
Psalm 121:5

STRONG AND COURAGEOUS

In the time of Jesus, the Israelites viewed the sea as the place of chaos — as the abyss where evil dwelt — which is why some theologians believe as few as 20 fishermen worked on the Sea of Galilee in that era. Anyone who chose to live and work on the water was considered to be courageous, and also slightly crazy. They got up each day and did the physically demanding work of fishing, and also had the emotional and spiritual courage to walk into the place of turmoil every day.

Of His twelve disciples, Jesus chose five fishermen . . . because He chooses people with the courage and strength to face chaos. If you're waking up to chaos today, know that Jesus believes you have what it takes to confront it with Him.

Jesus called out to them, "Come, follow me, and I will show you how to fish for people!"
Matthew 4:19, NLT

GETTING YOUR FEET WET

This is the Jordan River just outside of Jericho, a site most Christians know as the place where John baptized Jesus and where God's people entered the Promised Land. But for the Israelites of the Old Testament, the Jordan was a roadblock. Decades of irrigation have left the Jordan narrow today, but at the time of the Exodus, this was a wide, fast-flowing river that stopped the Israelites in their tracks. They were on the brink of a God-sized future, but were stuck at an obstacle. Do you ever feel like this? Like the thing God has for you is just out of reach?

God told the Israelites that the only way past the Jordan River was for them to take a step of faith into the water. He told them that only when their feet were wet would He stop the flow of the river — and this is exactly what happened. But in order for the river to stop where they were, God had to block it upstream. This means He was working long before His followers had worked up the courage and faith to move forward.

Are you facing an obstacle today? Are you stuck on the wrong side of your own "personal Jordan"? I believe that God is already working today to get you through your roadblock so He can move you from being grounded to being grateful.

For you will be treated as you treat others. The standard you use in judging is the standard by which you will be judged.
Matthew 7:2, NLT

WHAT IS IMPOSSIBLE FOR PEOPLE IS POSSIBLE WITH GOD

LUKE 18:27

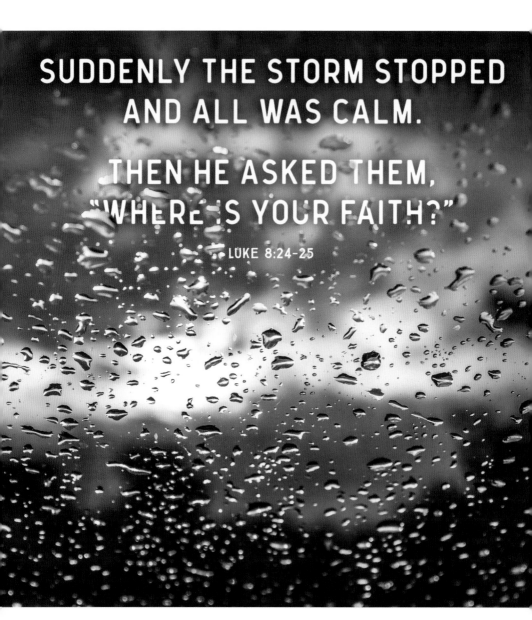

SUDDENLY THE STORM STOPPED AND ALL WAS CALM.

THEN HE ASKED THEM, "WHERE IS YOUR FAITH?"

LUKE 8:24-25

FACING THE STORM

There's a story in the Bible about a time when Jesus and His disciples crossed the Sea of Galilee in a huge storm. The rain and wind stirred up waves that nearly capsized the boat. The disciples were terrified … but Jesus was sleeping on a cushion in the stern of the boat. The disciples finally woke Jesus up, and He told the storm to "be quiet," and everything became calm. "Where is your faith?" Jesus then asked His followers (Luke 8:25).

I know how the disciples felt. When I'm facing a storm in life and Jesus seems silent, it's easy to panic. But after the storm has passed, I know He's asking me where my faith was. Even though Jesus was sleeping in the story, He was always in control — and He's in control of your life too! All He asks from us is that we have faith in Him.

Is your boat getting rocked today? Have faith that just like 2,000 years ago, Jesus can calm the storms in your life and give you peace.

The disciples went and woke him up, shouting, "Master, Master, we're going to drown!" When Jesus woke up, he rebuked the wind and the raging waves. Suddenly the storm stopped and all was calm. Then he asked them, "Where is your faith?" The disciples were terrified and amazed. "Who is this man?" they asked each other. "When he gives a command, even the wind and waves obey him!"
Luke 8:24–25, NLT

A PRAYERFUL INVITATION

These are the steps that lead down to Bells Beach on the Victorian surf coast of Australia. These steps are an invitation for surfers to ride some of the best waves in the world . . . and an invitation for tourists to come near to the waves and walk a beautiful, pristine coastline.

These steps remind me of prayer. You see, I used to treat prayer as nothing more than a time to ask God for things I wanted or to ask Him to do things I couldn't do for myself. But prayer is much more than that.

Abraham Joshua Heschel, a well-known rabbi, taught that prayer is "an invitation to God to intervene in our lives, to let His will prevail in our affairs; it is the opening of a window to Him in our will, an effort to make Him the Lord of our soul." It's more than asking God for things.

What would happen if you used prayer to invite God into your life instead of just asking for things?

Come near to God and he will come near to you. Wash your hands, you sinners, and purify your hearts, you double-minded.
James 4:8

GOING TO GOD'S HOUSE

Growing up in Australia, this is what I knew as the outback. It was flat. The ground was hard and barren. Temperatures in summer soared above 110 degrees Fahrenheit. The air was hot and dry. When the Bible describes the wilderness or desert of Israel, this is how I imagine it. Hot. Dry. Barren. Hard.

When life gets hard and barren, Christians often say they're "in the desert," like it's a bad thing, but the Bible says the desert is where God lives. The desert is where God spoke to Abraham, Moses, the Israelites, Isaiah, and on through Jesus. In fact, the Hebrew word for "desert" is *midbar*, which also means "the place of the word." And *midbar* shares the same Hebraic root as the word *debiyr*, which means the Holy of Holies — the place where God lives.

If you feel like you're in the desert today, you're closer to God than ever. Talk to a friend who is in the desert today.

I took care of you in the wilderness, in that dry and thirsty land.
Hosea 13:5, NLT

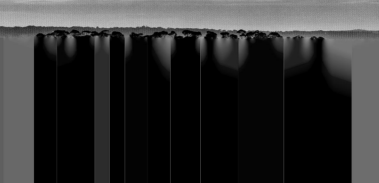

60

JOYFUL PRAISE

The word *hallelujah* has been used by followers of Jesus for centuries. This word is actually a combination of two Hebrew words that have great meaning.

The first word is *hallel*, which we translate as "praise," but which actually means so much more. It means to have such a deep and joyous praise and adoration for God that the ancient Jews required five complete psalms to define this word adequately. The second part is *Jah*, which simply means "God." So hallelujah literally means to joyfully, adoringly, and triumphantly praise God.

Will your words and actions today reflect joyful and triumphant praise?

Then I heard what sounded like a great multitude, like the roar of rushing waters and like loud peals of thunder, shouting: "Hallelujah! For our Lord God Almighty reigns."
Revelation 19:6

JOHN 14:26

THE HOLY SPIRIT

...

WILL REMIND YOU

...

OF ALL THINGS

DANCING FOR JOY

How often do you skim over parts of the Bible because what you read doesn't make sense or seem relevant?

A well-known Jewish rabbi named Akiba, who lived about 100 years after the time of Jesus, once said: "If you read a passage in the Bible and it doesn't apply to you today, dance for joy because you will need it someday, and then God will bring it back to you."

Could you, for the rest of the week, read a chapter of the Bible each day, and if you come to an idea that doesn't apply to you, take Akiba's advice and read it, then dance for joy, knowing that God will use this passage to encourage or challenge you in the future?

and the Comforter, the Holy Spirit, whom the Father will send in my name, he will teach you all things, and remind you of all things that I have said to you.
John 14:26 (Youngs)

DO YOU TRUST GOD?

A wise man once asked: "Can any one of you by worrying add a single hour to your life?" Great question!

God never said we'd have a problem-free existence . . . all He said was that we'd have everything we need for right now. I mean, if God cares so much for little things like flowers, surely He cares more for us, right? But despite this, the same wise man noted that all of us STILL worry about everything and anything — even what we will wear.

For a moment, right now, I want you to imagine what your life would be like if you trusted God like He wants you to trust Him.

Yet I tell you that not even Solomon in all his splendor was dressed like one of these.
Matthew 6:29

BUT WITH GOD
ALL THINGS ARE POSSIBLE

MATTHEW 19:26

WHAT ARE YOU CAPABLE OF?

If Jesus asked you to get out of THIS boat and walk on THIS water with Him, I bet you wouldn't hesitate. Let's be honest, when the waters are this smooth and calm, it's easy to take a step of faith. But when Jesus called Peter to step out of the safety of his boat, the story says the wind was so strong and the waves were so high that even the experienced fisherman was scared. Peter stepped out anyway, but then his fear took over and he sank. Jesus knew it was possible for Peter to walk on water, but Peter lost faith in what he was capable of with Jesus.

Jesus knows that you can do whatever He is calling you to do today . . . but you have to believe it. What could you achieve today if you refused to doubt, and simply believed what Jesus said — that with God, all things are possible?

Jesus looked at them and said, "With man this is impossible, but with God all things are possible."
Matthew 19:26

LAMENTATIONS 3:41

LET US LIFT OUR HEARTS
and our hands
TO GOD IN HEAVEN

A HUG FROM GOD

My youngest daughter has always had a passion for Jesus. When she prays, she assumes God hears her and will come through, and when she sings at church, she puts both hands high in the air and sings at the top of her lungs.

I once asked her why she puts her hands up when she sings, and she said: "When I sing to God and put my hands in the air, it's like I'm reaching for Him. And I imagine that He is reaching down for me at the same time, so He can pick me up and hug me." That's about the best picture of worship I've heard . . . and I love how she experiences God.

How do you experience God?

Let us lift up our hearts and our hands to God in heaven
Lamentations 3:41

PSALM 119:133

DIRECT MY

footsteps

ACCORDING

TO YOUR WORD

PRAY WITH YOUR FEET

There's an ancient Biblical teaching amongst the Jews that says all believers should "pray with your feet." The idea is that God designed each of us to answer the prayers of the people we're in community with by actively walking alongside them.

The rabbis taught this because they believed that while deep thought may change your behavior, deep behavior WILL change your thoughts.

Imagine if every Christian you know — including the one in the mirror — applied this idea today and started carrying each other's burdens.

Direct my footsteps according to your word; let no sin rule over me.
Psalm 119:133

PRACTICAL WISDOM

I used to think this verse meant that if I wanted to be wise, I had to memorize the Bible. I assumed that "wisdom" was the sort of head knowledge or insight only a few people have. But the Hebrew word for wisdom — *chokmah* — describes someone who has practical skills that help them thrive in life. So *chokmah* describes rabbis and teachers, but also skilled craftsmen, laborers, accountants, and artists.

As author Lois Tverberg says, "God's desire is that we have wisdom in all things in order to live the life He gave us to the very best." He gives us *chokmah* so we can be successful in teaching Scripture, studying for a test, repairing a car, balancing a budget, or painting.

How will you use your God-given wisdom today?

All wisdom comes from the LORD, and so do common sense and understanding.
Proverbs 2:6, CEV

ALL WISDOM
COMES FROM
The Lord
SO DO
COMMON SENSE
AND UNDERSTANDING
PROVERBS 2:6

A TREE OF LIFE

An old Jewish saying says that when you read and study the Bible it becomes "a tree of life to those that lay hold of it." I realized a few years ago that while I'd spent a lot of time looking at this "tree of life" and even sitting under its shade, I'd never really laid hold of it.

Throughout the Bible, Jesus says things like: "You have read in the Scriptures . . ." or "You have heard this . . ." because He assumed that His listeners read the Bible. But while the people listening to Him did know the Bible, most of us don't. Now, whenever I read Jesus saying these things, I stop reading, search for the verse or story He's referencing, read it, and THEN go back to read what Jesus said about it. Are you making the Bible a "tree of life"?

Wisdom is a tree of life to those who embrace her; happy are those who hold her tightly.
Proverbs 3:18, NLT

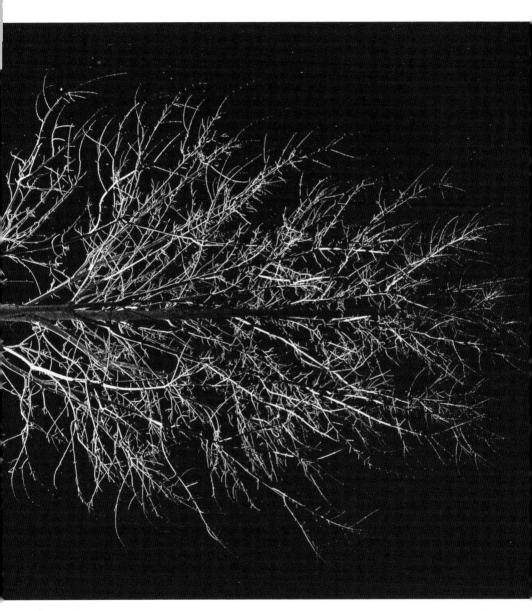

FEELING THE SQUEEZE

Is something in your life confining you or holding you captive? Is there something pressing in from all sides, restraining you and turning your life into a wreck? Perhaps it's a job or relationship. Maybe a need for money or status enslaves you. Are you imprisoned by an addiction or the pressure to live up to an image on social media?

There's a Hebrew term for this — *mitsrayim* — which is translated in the Bible as "Egypt," but which also means "narrow," "restricted," or "bondage." In the Bible, God frees His people from slavery in Egypt, but the story of the exodus is not just about a group of people being delivered from Egypt at a certain time in history. This story is also about God delivering and rescuing YOU from whatever is oppressing you and holding you captive TODAY!

Jesus said He came to set us free from the narrow places — the *mitsrayim* that confine us and wear us out.

The Spirit of the Lord is on me, because he has anointed me to proclaim good news to the poor. He has sent me to proclaim freedom for the prisoners and recovery of sight for the blind, to set the oppressed free."
Luke 4:18

STICKING TOGETHER

In chapter 22 of the book of Genesis, God promises Abraham, "I will certainly bless you. I will multiply your descendants beyond number, like the stars in the sky and the sand on the seashore" (v. 17). We read this as western Christians and think it's about numbers . . . but it's actually about community.

You see, Abraham knew two types of sand: the sand of the desert and the sand on the seashore. The desert sand is dry, so if you pick up a handful it slips through your fingers. The sand at the seashore, however, sticks together because it's kept wet by what the Jews would call the "living water" of the ocean. This is God's promise to Abraham. God designed His followers to be like sand at the seashore — to stick together and support each other through Jesus, who is the Living Water.

Who are the people sticking to you in community?

I will certainly bless you. I will multiply your descendants beyond number, like the stars in the sky and the sand on the seashore. Your descendants will conquer the cities of their enemies.
Genesis 22:17, NLT

LIGHT ON COMPASSION

In at least two accounts written about His life, Jesus says that when His followers show compassion to people in need, their bodies will be "full of light" (Matthew 6:21-23; Luke 11:33-36). Jesus wasn't pushing a new-age agenda. He was explaining that taking care of those around you is not just a nice habit to cultivate — it's central to our character as His followers.

Interestingly, the Hebrew word for light is *òwr*, which literally means "to bring order to something chaotic." In God's Kingdom, then, order is present when people who are in need or hurting are cared for by people who follow Jesus. When compassion for others is a central part of who we are as the Church, then and only then are our bodies full of light. And that light shines before the rest of the world and brings glory to God.

Are you ready to shine God's light by being compassionate today?

Keep your life as well-lighted as your best-lighted room.
Luke 11:36, MSG

AND WHO IS MY NEIGHBOR?

LUKE 10:29

83

Meet the Neighbors

When Jesus taught His followers to love their neighbor, someone asked Him: "And who is my neighbor?" (Luke 10:29). We assume our neighbors are the people we share a property line with, or the families living on our street or in our neighborhood. But Jesus said it's more than that.

He said our neighbor is anyone we come in contact with — even if they are nothing like us. Jesus said that even if they come from a different race, have opposing political or religious views, or live a lifestyle we disapprove of, we are to love them.

And we can't love our neighbors by just thinking nice things about them. If we're going to have any impact in loving our neighbors, we need to get to know them and learn how to love them.

How are you doing with this?

But he wanted to justify himself, so he asked Jesus, "And who is my neighbor?"
Luke 10:29

LIGHTING THE WAY

We all know that a lighthouse, like this one at Point Lonsdale in Australia, is used to warn boats about dangerous rocks or reefs and to let them know that the safety of land is near. Modern-day lighthouses are able to send out different kinds of light that mean different things to sailors, and they are precision-built to ensure the light and the message they send is understood and accurate.

If men are wise enough to provide lighthouses to guide ships at sea, it makes sense that God would provide something to help guide us through our lives. In Hebrew tradition, the Bible is often referred to as the *Torah Or*, which means "Guide of Light." They believe the Bible is designed to shine light in the darkness, guide against dangers, and lead the way to the safety and security of life with God.

Is the Bible your lighthouse?

The teaching of your word gives light, so even the simple can understand.
Psalm 119:130, NLT

THE TEACHING OF YOUR WORD GIVES LIGHT

PSALM 119:130

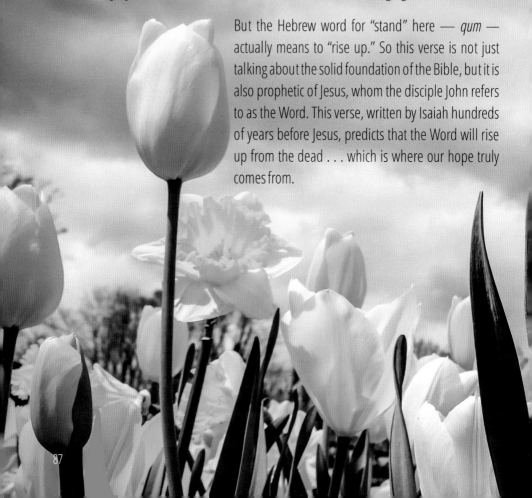

RISING TO A CHALLENGE

When Christians are going through a season of unexpected change, someone will invariably quote Isaiah 40:8: "The grass withers and the flowers fade, but the word of our God stands forever." They do it to remind us that we have a solid foundation in the Word of God — and it's encouraging to believe that God remains constant in an ever-changing world.

But the Hebrew word for "stand" here — *qum* — actually means to "rise up." So this verse is not just talking about the solid foundation of the Bible, but it is also prophetic of Jesus, whom the disciple John refers to as the Word. This verse, written by Isaiah hundreds of years before Jesus, predicts that the Word will rise up from the dead . . . which is where our hope truly comes from.

So no matter what you're experiencing today, you can draw hope from the resurrection of Jesus.

The grass withers and the flowers fade, but the word of our God stands forever."
Isaiah 40:8, *NLT*

LOVE
EACH OTHER AS I HAVE
LOVED YOU

JOHN 15:12

APPLYING YOUR FAITH

I took this photo early one morning in Australia when I noticed a person walking alone on the beach. It reminded me of the verse in the Bible that says Christians "walk by faith" (2 Corinthians 5:7, NASB). The Hebrew word for "walk" is *haliykah*, which specifically refers to how you apply the Scriptures in your life. The first followers of Jesus believed your *haliykah* was the most important part of your faith, because it directs the way you behave. For them, spiritual transformation started on the outside and worked its way in.

Jesus' *haliykah* was all about loving others. This is why He encouraged His followers with a "new commandment" to love each other (John 13:34). In fact, He said the world will know we are His followers by the way we love, care for, serve, encourage, and support the people around us.

Does the way you behave and live out your faith reflect Jesus' *haliykah*?

My command is this: Love each other as I have loved you.
John 15:12

WINGING IT

One of Israel's ancient prophets named Malachi prophesied that "the Sun of Righteousness will rise with healing in his wings" (Malachi 4:2). This verse didn't make sense to me until I learned that Sun of Righteousness is a name for the coming Messiah. The "wings" mentioned refers to the Hebrew word *kanaph*, which means "wings," but also means "corners," as in the corners of a garment or robe.

There's a story in the Gospels of Jesus going to a small town, where a woman who had been bleeding for 12 years understood this prophecy. She knew that she only needed to touch the *kanaph* of Jesus' robe to be healed.

For most reading these words, this may just be an interesting insight. But for someone reading this, you need to believe, like that woman did, that Jesus can heal you today.

But for you who fear my name, the Sun of Righteousness will rise with healing in his wings. And you will go free, leaping with joy like calves let out to pasture.
Malachi 4:2, NLT

REST IS HOLY

From my experience, the command to "remember the Sabbath day by keeping it holy" is the only one of the Ten Commandments that Christians brag about breaking. We don't tell our friends how well we lie or how much we covet . . . but we do say, "I'm SO busy!"; "I'm working 24/7!"; or my favorite, "I've got SO much going on right now." Am I right?

But God wants us to rest. He modeled rest. After a week of creating the Heavens and the Earth and everything that exists, God took a break. After literally making something out of nothing, on the seventh day God made nothing out of something. He created rest. God didn't rest because He was tired, He rested because He's holy. Rest is holy.

Will you make time to rest this weekend?

Then, because so many people were coming and going that they did not even have a chance to eat, he said to them, "Come with me by yourselves to a quiet place and get some rest."
Mark 6:31

93

ALL FIRED UP

One of my favorite passages in the Bible is Jeremiah 20:9, which reads: "But if I say, 'I will not mention his word or speak anymore in his name,' his word is in my heart like a fire, a fire shut up in my bones. I am weary of holding it in; indeed, I cannot." Whenever I read these words, I can sense the passion in Jeremiah's writing. This is a man with an intense excitement for God and the Scriptures.

Do you have this level of passion for God . . . or do you just attend church on the weekend and then resume normal life? Do you read the Bible out of joy or obligation?

I wish we all had a faith so passionate that there was no way we could contain it.

Imagine what the world — what your church — would be like if every follower of Jesus had such a compelling faith burning inside them that people wanted to be around them to experience it! What are you doing today to develop so much passion for God that you can't stop speaking of Him either in word or in the way you act?

But if I say, "I will not mention his word or speak anymore in his name," his word is in my heart like a fire, a fire shut up in my bones. I am weary of holding it in; indeed, I cannot.
Jeremiah 20:9

BEAUTY IN EVERYTHING

The first followers of Jesus believed that God was everywhere and in everything. They would say that God was in every moment of their day, in every interaction, in every breath . . . in everything. If this is true, then as Christians, the challenge for us is to actually experience the beauty of God in everything.

Perhaps this is what the apostle Paul meant when he wrote, "I pray that the eyes of your heart may be enlightened in order that you may know the hope to which he has called you" (Ephesians 1:18). Are your eyes opened to see the hope of God in every moment?

Imagine what today would be like if you experienced Jesus in every breath, every moment, every conversation, every meal, every meeting, every tear . . . in everything.

I pray that the eyes of your heart may be enlightened in order that you may know the hope to which he has called you, the riches of his glorious inheritance in his holy people.
Ephesians 1:18

HEBREWS 11:30

IT WAS BY FAITH THAT

THE PEOPLE OF ISRAEL
...
MARCHED AROUND JERIC[O]
...
AND THE WALLS

CAME CRASHING DOWN

WILL YOU FOLLOW?

God told the Israelites that if they marched around the wall of Jericho once a day for six days, and then seven times on the seventh day, the wall would fall down (Joshua 6). Why did He do that? Couldn't God knock the wall down Himself?

The marching was not about the wall, it was about the people. God could have destroyed that wall in the blink of an eye … but He wanted the people's obedience. God wanted to know that His people would follow Him no matter what. He wants the same from us, too.

God is asking you to start, stop, or change something today . . . and He wants your obedience because He cares more about your heart than your situation.

It was by faith that the people of Israel marched around Jericho for seven days, and the walls came crashing down.
Hebrews 11:30, NLT

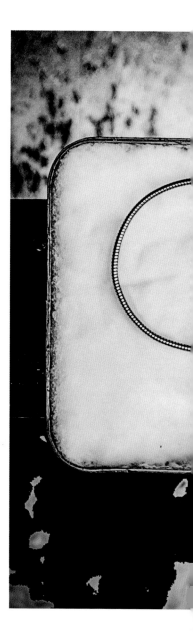

"COLD CALLING" GOD

How often do we use prayer as nothing more than an emergency call or a "cold call" to God?

Too often we only pray when we need or want something from God, which is understandable considering that the English word "pray" means "ask or beg." But the Hebrew word for prayer — *tephillah* — means "self evaluate." So to the Jews of the Bible, prayer was not a time when they asked God for things . . . it was a time when they examined themselves. They would use prayer as a way to compare their actions, behavior, and attitude against God's holiness. Will this idea change the way you pray today?

Test yourselves to make sure you are solid in the faith. Don't drift along taking everything for granted. Give yourselves regular checkups. You need firsthand evidence, not mere hearsay, that Jesus Christ is in you.
2 Corinthians 13:5–6, MSG

BE LIKE YOUR RABBI

In Jesus' day, a disciple was with his rabbi 24/7. He watched how his rabbi treated the poor, handled money, ate food, and what he did when he was sad, angry, or happy. Every activity was an opportunity to learn how to be like the rabbi.

In the four Gospels we can learn all these things about Jesus, but when was the last time you read them all, in order, front to back? I was once challenged: "If you can't find time to read all the Gospels every month, you can't call yourself a disciple."

So . . . when was the last time you read all four Gospels?

Whoever claims to live in him must live as Jesus did.
1 John 2:6

THE LORD GOD
BREATHED THE
Breath of Life
INTO HIS NOSTRILS AND THE MAN
BECAME A LIVING BEING
GENESIS 2:7

INHALE SPIRIT, EXHALE PRAISE

We don't often think about breathing . . . unless we're running out of air. But breath is an important theme throughout the Bible. The Book of Genesis says God made man from mud and put skin, muscles, bones, blood vessels, tendons, veins, and hair in place, but the man was not a "living being" until God breathed into his body.

The word for "breath" in Hebrew is *ruwach*, which also means "Spirit," so man only becomes a "living being" when God gives him His Spirit. According to the Psalms, "everything that has breath praise[s] the LORD" (Psalm 150:6), so to be alive we first inhale God's Spirit and then we exhale praise. Inhale Spirit, exhale praise. This is life.

Do you have this rhythm in your life?

Then the LORD God formed a man from the dust of the ground and breathed into his nostrils the breath of life, and the man became a living being.
Genesis 2:7

GOD-BREATHED INSPIRATION

Every artist gets their inspiration from somewhere. Most of my inspiration comes from nature. I see a scene like this on the Australian surf coast and get drawn to the idea of capturing it as authentically and beautifully as possible.

But did you know that the word *inspiration* comes from the Greek *theopneustos*, which means "God-breathed"? Thus the original idea of being "inspired" was that God's Spirit would move a person to do something creative. When someone talks of being inspired, whether they know it or not, they are speaking about having the Spirit of God influence them.

Today, you may feel like your life is ordinary, mundane, and uninspiring, but anything you do can be God-breathed ... if you seek Him.

But there is a spirit in man: and the inspiration of the Almighty gives them understanding.
Job 32:8, *KJV*

JOB 32:8

THE INSPIRATION OF
THE ALMIGHTY
GIVES THEM UNDERSTANDING

SURRENDERING TO GOD

There's a verse in *The Message* version of the Bible that reads, "God proves to be good to the man who passionately waits, to the woman who diligently seeks. It's a good thing to quietly hope, quietly hope for help from God" (Lamentations 3:26). We define the word *wait* as staying where we are or delaying action . . . but in Hebrew the word *qavah* means to gather together with God. So this verse means that we will find hope when we passionately "gather together" with God.

The rabbis would teach that gathering together with God happens when we choose to follow Him and surrender to Him. This is what it means to wait and hope for help from God.

I'm praying for everyone who reads these words and is waiting on God today.

It's a good thing to quietly hope, quietly hope for help from GOD. It's a good thing when you're young to stick it out through the hard times.
Lamentations 3:26–27, MSG

LIVE A BIG LIFE

At over a kilometer long and 42 stories high, the Sydney Harbour Bridge is big, expansive, and high-capacity . . . a lot like God's plan for your life. When Jesus said His followers would "have life and have it abundantly" (John 10:10, ESV), the Greek word for "abundantly" is *perissos*, which literally means "beyond measure, big, expansive, and with a huge capacity."

Having the kind of big, expansive life God has placed in your heart doesn't come from sitting around waiting for your big break — it comes from being faithful in the small

111

things, like serving those in need, loving the people on the fringe, studying God's Word, and learning to be like Jesus. You want the big life God promised? Let Him work with you in the small things first.

The thief comes only to steal and kill and destroy. I came that they may have life and have it abundantly.
John 10:10, ESV

When my wife and I saw this red sky over our backyard in Georgia, we called our girls to see it too, because we were in awe. We were in awe of the colors, the shapes, and the God who created this spectacular scene.

The Hebrew word we translate as "awe" is *yir'ah*, which means "respect, reverence, and worship." *Yir'ah* also means "fear." I grew up thinking to "fear the Lord" meant being afraid of Him, but as we watched this stunning sunset, I didn't feel fear. I felt awe and reverence. I felt *yir'ah*.

Having the type of awe and reverence for God that motivates us to do His will is the beginning of wisdom. Do you fear the Lord today?

The fear of the LORD is the beginning of knowledge, but fools despise wisdom and instruction.
Proverbs 1:7

PREPARING THE SOIL

My family lives near some beautiful farmland in north Georgia. Whenever I drive past, I'm always amazed by a farmer's ability to prepare soil, plant seeds, and harvest crops. The farmer can't make corn come out of a stalk or tomatoes come out of a vine — God takes care of that. Likewise, we can't produce faith in our family and friends. We can't make people believe. What we can do is create the best possible environment in which faith can grow.

We need to love the people around us. As my friend Jeff Henderson says, "For too long the church has been known for what it is against, not what it's for." If you love the family, friends, and neighbors around you, accept them, serve them, and show them a transformed life. In this way you create the right soil so God can work with them.

So neither the one who plants nor the one who waters is anything, but only God, who makes things grow.
1 Corinthians 3:7

FOR THE WORD OF GOD
IS ALIVE AND POWERFUL

HEBREWS 4:12

A STEADY STREAM

There's an old Jewish story about a rabbi who was walking near his house when he noticed the way a small stream of water had carved a deep impression into a massive boulder through years of erosion. "If mere water can do this to a hard rock, how much more can God's Word carve into my heart of flesh?" the rabbi said.

If water had hit the rock all at once, the rock would have been unchanged. But a constant and steady stream of water over many years was able to completely transform the stone.

In the same way, when we're consistently reading God's Word, praying, worshiping, and being generous day after day, year after year, God is able to shape us.

For the word of God is alive and powerful. It is sharper than the sharpest two-edged sword, cutting between soul and spirit, between joint and marrow. It exposes our innermost thoughts and desires.
Hebrews 4:12, NLT

WHEN GOD STARTS SOMETHING ...

In the opening scene of the book of Genesis, we see three things: water, the Spirit hovering, and God's voice. All three of these were present when God began something new on the earth.

These things are together again in the Gospels, when Jesus comes up out of the baptismal waters. The skies open and Jesus sees God's Spirit in the form of a dove. He then hears God's voice coming from the clouds, saying, "This is my beloved Son . . . listen to him" (Matthew 17:5, ESV).

Water, the Spirit hovering, and God's voice. All three at the beginning of creation and all three at the beginning of Jesus' ministry. The first was God creating the world . . . the second time was Jesus creating a new life for all who follow Him.

While he was still speaking, a bright cloud covered them, and a voice from the cloud said, "This is my Son, whom I love; with him I am well pleased. Listen to him!"
Matthew 17:5

AS IRON SHARPENS IRON,
SO A FRIEND SHARPENS A FRIEND.

PROVERBS 27:17

121

WHO ARE YOU WALKING WITH?

The Hebrew word *haver* describes someone who partners with a friend to enhance their learning. *Haver* is the picture of two people walking their spiritual journey together and helping each other wrestle with their faith. The book of Proverbs would describe this relationship as iron sharpening iron.

A famous rabbinic quote from Jesus' day said that every believer should "acquire for yourself a rabbi, and get an *haver*" if they wanted to get close to God.

Who is your *haver*? Do you have one?

As iron sharpens iron, so a friend sharpens a friend.
Proverbs 27:17, NLT

HOW BIG ARE YOUR CORNERS?

In the days of the Bible, your neighbors could see how much faith you had by looking over your fence to see the size of your corners. In the book of Leviticus, God told His people to leave the corners of their land uncut at harvest so the poor could pick the leftover grain and have food to eat. People who were generous had big corners on their land, while those who didn't believe God could provide for them had small corners because they harvested close to the edge of their land.

If we looked over your fence, what would we see? Do you have faith that God will provide for you today? Are you generous to those around you who are in need?

How big are your corners?

When you reap the harvest of your land, moreover, you shall not reap to the very corners of your field nor gather the gleaning of your harvest; you are to leave them for the needy and the alien. I am the LORD your God.
Leviticus 23:22, NASB

A JAR OF LIGHTS

Jesus challenged His followers to be a light to those around us, pointing them toward God. God decided His message to the world would be spoken through YOU! How you live, act, and speak should attract people to God in the same way a moth is attracted to light.

But rather than your life being one single light shining the way to God, what if it's actually a string of smaller lights — with every action, word, and decision building on the other until your life is like a jar of lights? It still shines brightly and it still leads people to God . . . one word, one step at a time.

Today, I pray that with every word, every step, every decision, every breath your faith will shine brightly to those around you.

You are the light of the world. A town built on a hill cannot be hidden. Neither do people light a lamp and put it under a bowl. Instead they put it on its stand, and it gives light to everyone in the house. In the same way, let your light shine before others, that they may see your good deeds and glorify your Father in heaven.
Matthew 5:14–16

BLESSED IS THE ONE WHO TRUSTS IN THE LORD...

THEY WILL BE LIKE A TREE PLANTED BY THE WATER

THAT SENDS OUT ITS ROOTS BY THE STREAM.

JEREMIAH 17:7, 8

SURVIVING DIFFICULT TIMES

This is an acacia tree in the desert of Israel. This tree has been designed by God to survive decades of intense heat and drought. It can survive tough circumstances because it has a deep root system to sustain it during the hardest of times. Even during a time of drought, this tree is still able to bless local residents by providing shade during the day and wood for fire at night.

This is the tree the prophet Jeremiah had in mind when he wrote, "Blessed is the one who trusts in the LORD, whose confidence is in him. They will be like a tree planted by the water that sends out its roots by the stream" (Jeremiah 17:7-8). God has specifically designed the acacia to survive difficult times, and He has designed you to be like the acacia — to survive the harshest of circumstances and bless others through hard times. But this only happens when the foundations of your faith are deep.

Are you going through a tough time today? Are you in the middle of a drought? I believe God wants you to develop deep-rooted trust and faith in Him — not just to survive your own circumstances, but to also bless others around you with your confidence in God.

You are already clean because of the word I have spoken to you.
John 15:3

JESUS IS YOUR EXAMPLE,
AND YOU MUST
FOLLOW IN HIS STEPS.

1 PETER 2:21

WALKING THE BIBLE

Author Peter Enns once wrote that the Bible is "a land we get to know by hiking through it and exploring its many paths and terrains. This land is both inviting and inspiring, but also unfamiliar, odd, and at points unsettling — even risky and precarious." I love this image!

Experienced hikers know you never walk an unfamiliar path alone, and you shouldn't read the Bible alone either. You need people with you on your spiritual journey who can help you navigate the terrain. You also need mentors who are further up the trail to act as guides.

As you step forward into the Bible today, my prayer is that your boots would be covered in the dust of your rabbi Jesus as you walk closely behind Him.

For God called you to do good, even if it means suffering, just as Christ suffered for you. He is your example, and you must follow in his steps.
1 Peter 2:21, NLT

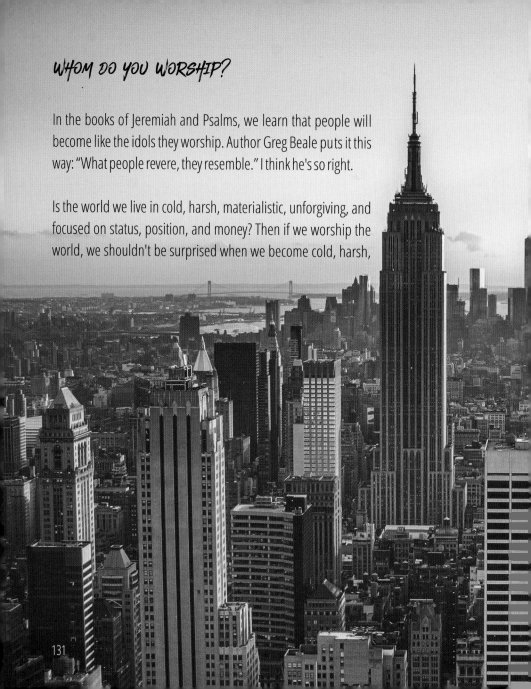

WHOM DO YOU WORSHIP?

In the books of Jeremiah and Psalms, we learn that people will become like the idols they worship. Author Greg Beale puts it this way: "What people revere, they resemble." I think he's so right.

Is the world we live in cold, harsh, materialistic, unforgiving, and focused on status, position, and money? Then if we worship the world, we shouldn't be surprised when we become cold, harsh,

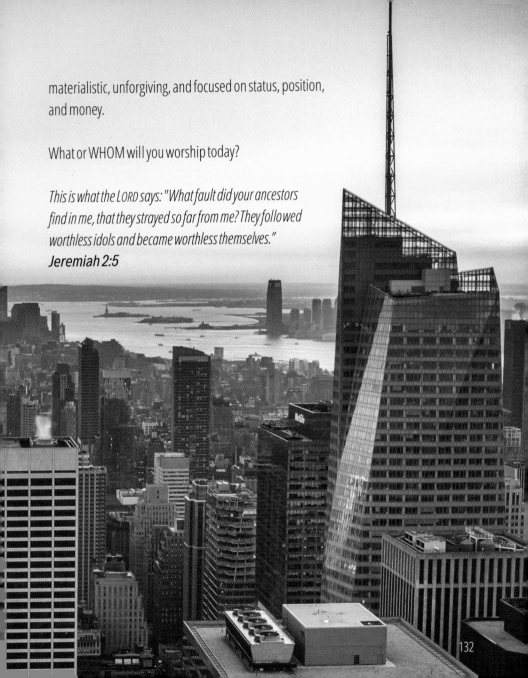

materialistic, unforgiving, and focused on status, position, and money.

What or WHOM will you worship today?

This is what the LORD says: "What fault did your ancestors find in me, that they strayed so far from me? They followed worthless idols and became worthless themselves."
Jeremiah 2:5

A REED OR AN OAK?

When Jesus described John the Baptist to a crowd of people, He said that John was not a "weak reed, swayed by every breath of wind" (Matthew 11:7, NLT). This image came from a Jewish parable about a reed and an oak tree planted by a river. The oak tree has deep roots that allow it to stand strong even in a powerful gale, but a reed twists and bends with the wind to avoid being blown over. The point of the parable is that a reed compromises, but an oak stands firm, so Jesus was describing John as a man defined by his strong faith, values, and moral convictions.

Whenever you are indecisive, whenever you conform, when you compromise your beliefs or bend your values ... you're more like a reed than an oak.

How would Jesus describe you?

So he replied to the messengers, "Go back and report to John what you have seen and heard: The blind receive sight, the lame walk, those who have leprosy are cleansed, the deaf hear, the dead are raised, and the good news is proclaimed to the poor. Blessed is anyone who does not stumble on account of me."

Luke 7:22–23

BLESSED IS ANYONE

who does not stumble

ON ACCOUNT OF ME

LUKE 7:23

WHERE ARE YOU PLANTED?

You can't grow coconuts in Alaska. Coconuts grow on palm trees, and palm trees grow best in tropical climates with warm, salty air and plenty of sunlight. If you want to produce a certain type of fruit, you've got to plant the tree in the right atmosphere where it can grow to maturity. It's the same with every follower of Jesus.

For our faith to produce fruit, we need to be planted in the house of the Lord, where we "flourish," according to Psalm 92:12. Being planted in God's house means regularly attending and participating in a church community.

Are you planted so you can grow to maturity?

Those that be planted in the house of the LORD shall flourish in the courts of our God.
Psalm 92:13, KJV

YOUR LIVING TESTIMONY

Sunsets remind me of Psalm 19, where David writes, "The heavens proclaim the glory of God. . . . They speak without a sound or word; their voice is never heard. Yet their message has gone throughout the earth" (Psalm 19:1, 3-4, NLT). Have you ever considered that your life is supposed to send this same message? In several places in the Bible we're told to love God with "all our soul," a phrase that uses the Hebrew word *nephesh*, which means "soul" and also means "life." In other words, we're supposed to love God WITH all our life FOR all our life. This is not loving Him for an hour each week at church — it's loving Him in everything we do in every minute of every day.

If you never spoke another word, would the way you live your life glorify God before the world?

How clearly the sky reveals God's glory! How plainly it shows what he has done!
Psalm 19:1, GNT

HOW CLEARLY TH
PSALM 19:1

SKY REVEALS GOD'S GLORY

FOLLOWING THE STOPS OF JESUS

A few years ago I spent a weekend fishing in upstate New York. I'd get up before dawn, row across the stillness of the water, and fish for hours. In those moments before the sun came up, I was fully aware of the serenity. Have you ever noticed that it's only when you slow down that you realize just how busy you are?

Jesus had a rhythm of doing a season of ministry, and then resting. He would speak to large crowds or heal a group of people, and then take time off. The disciples wanted Him to maintain His momentum, but Jesus would say no and rest instead. As Christians, we too often get so caught up in following the STEPS of Jesus that we miss the STOPS of Jesus.

How will you follow the STOPS of Jesus today?

The LORD replied, "My Presence will go with you, and I will give you rest."
Exodus 33:14

MY PRESENCE
WILL GO
WITH YOU,
AND I WILL
GIVE YOU REST

EXODUS 33:14

MATTHEW 4:19

COME, FOLLOW

COVERED IN HIS DUST

Jesus didn't hand His disciples a textbook. He didn't enroll them in a course or give them a devotional. He simply invited them to follow Him, live life beside Him, and learn from Him. From this method of teaching came a well-known saying that you learn from your rabbi by "covering yourself in his dust." The idea is that you follow so closely behind him as he walks that the dust from your rabbi's feet clings to your clothes. When you follow your rabbi closely, your heart changes.

Can you imagine what your day would be like if you followed Jesus' example and teaching so closely that you were covered in His dust?

"Come, follow me," Jesus said, "and I will send you out to fish for people."
Matthew 4:19

GIVE THANKS
IN EVERY CIRCUMSTANCE

1 THESSALONIANS 5:18

WHAT ARE YOU THANKFUL FOR?

When was the last time you thanked God for the sunset? Have you ever thanked God for thunder or blessed Him for the trees?

The first followers of Jesus had a system of short blessings called *berachot* that they used to thank God every day. I think modern Christians often forget to be thankful, and as my friend Andy Stanley says, "It's not enough to feel gratitude, you've got to express it." So tonight, as you watch the sun set, say these ancient words: "Blessed are you, the Lord our God, ruler of the universe who speaks the evening into being and arranges the stars in their place. Blessed are you, Lord who brings on the evening." Let these words give you an attitude of gratitude.

What are you thankful to God for today?

Give thanks in all circumstances; for this is God's will for you in Christ Jesus.
1 Thessalonians 5:18

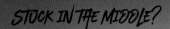

STUCK IN THE MIDDLE?

When I took this photo on a beautiful Saturday morning in Georgia, I was thinking about what the Saturday after Jesus died was like. History says Jesus died on Friday and rose on Sunday, which means that Saturday in between is the only day in 2000+ years when no one on earth believed Jesus was alive.

But that dark day was the middle part of a three-day story that recurs throughout Scripture. From Abraham and Isaac to Rahab and Esther . . . something bad happens on day one, but on day three God provides a way out. He did with Jesus' resurrection, too.

Are you in the middle of a three-day story today? You lost your job. Your marriage is in turmoil. You're getting kicked out. The test results

were bad. If that's you, remember that Sunday is coming! God will provide a way!

For what I received I passed on to you as of first importance: that Christ died for our sins according to the Scriptures, that he was buried, that he was raised on the third day according to the Scriptures.
1 Corinthians 15:3–4

GETTING TO KNOW GOD

From the time I first started following Jesus, I assumed I was supposed to study the stories in the Bible to learn, intellectually, about God and His nature. But the first followers of Jesus learned these stories to become familiar with God through a relationship and experience.

This is a photo of a small section of the Big Creek Greenway trail near my house in Georgia. I could tell you that this trail runs for more than 13 miles through Forsyth County in Georgia and attracts hundreds of runners, cyclists, and walkers every day. It runs through swamps, national parks, and alongside creeks. This is an intellectual explanation of the trail . . . but there's more to it than that. To really understand it, you need to experience it. You need to feel the coolness of the air through the national forest, jog over the wooden boardwalks, cycle up the inclines and over the winding bridges. You need to say good morning to passersby and walk dogs on leashes that are a little too long. This is when you "know" the Big Creek Greenway trail.

It's the same with God. Knowing about Him and experiencing Him are two different things. Today, try to read God's Word with the goal of developing a deeper relationship with Him and to have an experience of Him — not just learn something about Him.

The LORD is near to all who call on him, to all who call on him in truth.
Psalm 145:18

GROWING YOUR FAITH

This field near my family's house in Australia looks full of life and color, but these flowers are actually a pest. These wild canola flowers may look pretty, but they're overrunning and destroying the native ecosystem. It reminds me of the way bad habits and sin can creep into our lives because they look good, but then they choke and strangle life.

It's like the story Jesus once told about a farmer planting seed. Some seed fell amongst thorns that choked and killed the plants (Mark 4:4). Sometimes the thing that's dragging us away from God looks pretty and full of life, but it's actually destroying our faith.

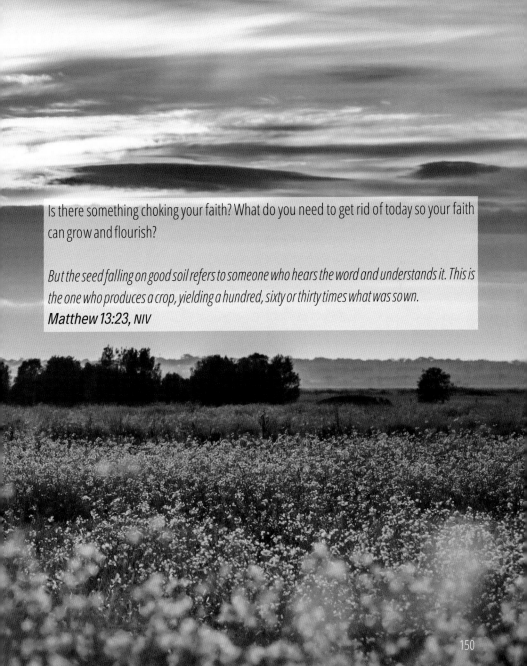

Is there something choking your faith? What do you need to get rid of today so your faith can grow and flourish?

But the seed falling on good soil refers to someone who hears the word and understands it. This is the one who produces a crop, yielding a hundred, sixty or thirty times what was sown.
Matthew 13:23, NIV

ON THE OTHER SIDE

I photographed this amazing fisherman on the pier in Malibu. While I'd never dream of giving him fishing advice, there's a story of Jesus once telling professional fishermen to stop what they were doing and cast their nets on the "right-hand side of the boat" (John 21:6, NLT). When they did, they caught 153 large fish! Have you ever wondered why we're told they caught exactly 153 fish?

The Jews believed there were 153 pagan nations on the other side of the Sea of Galilee, so when Jesus told them to throw their nets on the other side, He was telling them to spread His gospel to new people who hadn't heard His message yet.

Have you shared your faith with the same family and friends over and over? Perhaps Jesus is telling you that it's time to try the other side of your boat at work or school or at home.

He said, "Throw your net on the right side of the boat and you will find some." When they did, they were unable to haul the net in because of the large number of fish.
John 21:6

THOUGH THE MOUNTAINS BE SHAKEN
YET MY UNFAILING LOVE FOR YOU WILL NOT BE SHAKEN

ISAIAH 54:10

GOD'S KINDNESS

Whenever I photograph mountains like these in north Georgia, a verse in the Book of Isaiah comes to mind that reads: "Though the mountains be shaken and the hills be removed, yet my unfailing love for you will not be shaken" (Isaiah 54:10). The Hebrew word translated as "love" here is *hesed* (or *checed*), which is a hard word to define. Theologian John Oswalt says *hesed* is "a completely undeserved kindness and generosity." *Hesed* is not just a feeling, it's an action. It "intervenes on behalf of loved ones and comes to their rescue," according to Lois Tverberg.

Hesed is not romantic love. It's faithful. It's reliable. It's a wife praying for years for her husband to know God. It's a dad once again bailing out his drug-addicted son. It's parents who lovingly, daily care for their autistic child.

Today, you can rely on God's *hesed* for you no matter what you face.

"Though the mountains be shaken and the hills be removed, yet my unfailing love for you will not be shaken nor my covenant of peace be removed," says the LORD, who has compassion on you.
Isaiah 54:10

WALK WITH THE WISE

The Bible often describes your life as being a path that you walk along. There are lots of verses about this, but my favorite is in the book of Proverbs: "The path of the righteous is like the light of dawn, which shines brighter and brighter until full day" (Proverbs 4:18, ESV). We all want a path that shines bright, but for many of us, our path seems dark and lonely.

The author of Proverbs tells us that we can become wise by walking with the wise (Proverbs 13:20). In order to walk the path of the righteous that shines like the light of dawn, you need

155

a wise mentor helping to guide you.

Do you have a wise mentor? Do you have someone walking alongside you on your spiritual journey?

But the path of the righteous is like the light of dawn, which shines brighter and brighter until full day.
Proverbs 4:18, ESV

WALKING BY FAITH

There's a place in Tennessee called Ruby Falls, a spectacular natural waterfall that flows 1,120 feet underneath a mountain range. To get to the waterfall, you go underground 260 feet in an elevator and then hike nearly a mile on a slippery trail through dark caverns, low ceilings, and stalactite rock formations until you're at a depth that is almost the height of the Empire State Building. Then the cavern opens up to reveal this glorious, rainwater-fed 145-foot high waterfall. It's stunning.

Life is sometimes like a visit to Ruby Falls. Sometimes you find yourself in a dark place where you bump your head, lose your footing, and feel like you're going down. But if you have faith to keep walking, you find something glorious that only God could orchestrate.

Is life dark and slippery today? Keep walking, because God has something glorious to reveal to you.

The light shines in the darkness, and the darkness can never extinguish it.
John 1:5, NLT

THE TREE OF LIFE

The word for "tree" used throughout the first Greek translation of the Bible is *dendron*. For example, a fig tree would have been translated as a "fig dendron." The Tree of Life would have been the "Dendron of Life." It's this way throughout the Bible, except when referring to the cross of Christ. When referring to the cross, the Greek translators used the word for a "cursed tree," which is *xylon*. So Jesus was nailed to a *xylon*.

It's interesting that when the disciple John wrote the book of Revelation, he used the word *xylon* to describe the Tree of Life he saw in the new heaven, the leaves of which would "heal the nations" (Revelation 22:2). So John suggests that the Tree of Life in the middle of God's new heaven is the same cursed tree of Jesus' crucifixion.

I wonder what this does for your picture of heaven?

Whoever has ears, let them hear what the Spirit says to the churches. To the one who is victorious, I will give the right to eat from the tree of life, which is in the paradise of God.
Revelation 2:7

WHAT'S IN THE WAY OF GOD?

This is Juan, a boy I met on a mission trip in El Salvador. Juan lives in a mud-brick house that has branches for a roof and an oil drum with a hot plate as an oven. Juan doesn't have an iPhone. He doesn't have a bike or a TV. He doesn't have any of the things we take for granted.

What Juan does have is an understanding that God loves him and provides all that he needs. He doesn't have anything to get in the way of his relationship with God. He doesn't have any distractions. It's just him and God. Maybe that's why he's so happy.

Unlike Juan, I often let things like work, money concerns, social status, relationships, and TV distract me from God. Some of those things are good, but not if we let them get in the way of what God knows is best.

[Let us fix] our eyes on Jesus, the pioneer and perfecter of faith. For the joy set before him he endured the cross, scorning its shame, and sat down at the right hand of the throne of God.
Hebrews 12:2, *NIV*

WHATEVER YOU DO,
DO IT ALL FOR THE GLORY OF GOD.

1 CORINTHIANS 10:31

WORSHIP AS YOU WORK

This is how most of us picture worship. Worship has become the first part of a church service when people sing. People think of it as a style of music. But there's more to it than that. One Hebrew word for "worship" is *ábad*, which means "to sing" but also means "to serve or work." In the story of the Exodus, Moses tells Pharaoh that God's people need to go to *ábad* God. The word here gets translated as either "worship" or "serve" (Exodus 8:20). When God tells the people about the Sabbath, He says, "Six days you shall *ábad*, but on the seventh day you shall rest" (Exodus 20:9). Here *ábad* is translated as "work."

You see, God does not want us to worship Him just one day of the week . . . He wants us to serve and worship Him (*ábad*) every day, even as we work (*ábad*)!

Whether you're at your home, office, or classroom today, God says you can ábad — work, serve, and worship — for His glory. Everything you do is a reflection of the God you serve.

So whether you eat or drink or whatever you do, do it all for the glory of God.
1 Corinthian 10:31

DO YOU OVERLOOK JESUS?

There's a story in the Bible about Jesus healing a blind man by spitting in his eyes, but he isn't completely healed at first. The man sees, but everything is blurry and the people around him look like trees (Mark 8:24). Was Jesus having an "off" day?

This story comes right after Jesus feeds 4,000 people with seven loaves of bread, which happens after He feeds 5,000 people with five loaves. Then Jesus hears the disciples arguing about the amount of food they have with them, and He is like, "You've got to be kidding me!" So He has them pull the boat over, grabs a blind man, and heals him just enough so that he has eyes, but fails to truly see. Jesus is saying that His followers are like this — they have seen Jesus perform miracles, but they still don't see Him in their everyday life.

How often are you so focused on your day that you overlook what Jesus did for you yesterday?

I will praise the LORD at all times. I will constantly speak his praises.
Psalm 34:1, NLT

I WILL PRAISE THE LORD AT ALL TIMES

PSALM 34:1

GOD'S MOST TREASURED PLACE

In the ancient Middle East, when two people made a contract or covenant, they would always make two copies of the agreement and each person would store their copy in their most sacred, treasured place. When God made a covenant with Moses, He wrote two copies on stone tablets. One copy was placed in the Ark of the Covenant inside the Holy of Holies—Israel's most sacred place. The other copy was for Moses and the people of Israel — God's most sacred place.

Over the centuries, man's sacred places have become elaborate churches, but God doesn't want His covenant stored inside ornate buildings. In the book of Hebrews, we read that God deliberately put His new covenant in the place that is most holy and most cherished to Him: your heart.

YOU are God's most sacred and treasured place. He stores His Word in YOUR HEART because He wants YOU to live it out each day in the way you act and speak.

This is the covenant I will establish with the people of Israel after that time, declares the Lord. I will put my laws in their minds and write them on their hearts. I will be their God, and they will be my people.
Hebrews 8:10

IS THERE A HOLE IN YOUR WALL?

Do you ever feel like it's hard to take care of your spiritual journey every day? In Philippians we read that we should "take an interest in others, too" (Philippians 2:4, NLT). How can we do that if we're barely keeping up ourselves?

The Jews in Jesus' day understood what it meant to care for yourself and others because they did this in their gardens. Gardens were groups of terraced land stacked side-by-side on a hillside. Each plot was separated by a stone wall and belonged to a different family. But if one family neglected their wall, a heavy rain could wash away their garden AND the gardens on either side and below theirs. So families worked together to repair each others' walls to

ensure that every garden was strong.

When they cared about the hole in someone else's wall, their wall was stronger. Likewise, when we care for the spiritual journey of others in our community, our whole community is made stronger. Whose wall are you caring for today?

Don't look out only for your own interests, but take an interest in others, too.
Philippians 2:4, NLT

MERCY AND COMPASSION

There's a verse in the Bible that talks about God's mercies being "new every morning" (Lamentations 3:23). The word "mercy" here is the Hebrew word *rachum*, which means "to actively show compassion." So this verse means that every morning, God actively shows compassion toward us.

The first believers used to teach that every night our soul goes back to God to be given wisdom and be close to its Creator . . . and then God returns it every morning so we can begin a new day. While this is a great picture of God's compassion toward us, I know some of us find it hard to start a new day because we still carry the troubles of the previous day and don't feel we deserve God's compassion. Or maybe you're like me and wake up some mornings feeling like the bad things that happened in your past will overwhelm you in the day ahead. To this, my friend Andy Stanley says, "There is an appropriate way to use your story, not as an excuse but as a testimony to God's ability to free you from your past." That is God's mercy and compassion!

As the sun rises this morning, may you be aware of God's tangible compassion and mercy toward you.

And God said, "Let there be light," and there was light.
Genesis 1:3

FACING YOUR STORM

When Jesus said, "Here on earth you will have many trials and sorrows. But take heart, because I have overcome the world," (John 16:33, NLT), He gave His followers peace and hope even when storm clouds are brewing in our lives. The word we translate as "take heart" is the word *chazaq*, which is a call to action that means "to behave with courage and urgency." Jesus is telling us to confidently face the storms of life because He has already overcome the world. In Jesus' day, faith was not something you believed, it was something you did. So in this verse, Jesus is calling us to put our faith into action. Your life doesn't get transformed by chance, it gets transformed by choice. *Chazaq* means to choose to step forward with courage. Are you facing a storm in life today? Then today is the day you need to step forward and seize the moment with courageous faith.

"I have told you these things, so that in me you may have peace. In this world you will have trouble. But take heart! I have overcome the world."
John 16:33

WHAT IS JESUS HINTING AT?

Landscape photographers will tell you that some of the best sunrise photographs come when you can't even see the sun. When there's just a hint of sun peeking through clouds, the light can create the most stunning colors. In the same way, some of Jesus' most amazing teaching came when He didn't quote a Bible verse, but just hinted at it.

This is a Jewish teaching technique known as *remez* that rabbis used to increase the impact of a lesson. They would quote a part of Scripture and let people fill in the blank and deduce the lesson themselves. Jesus did this when He told us to forgive people up to "77 times." We assume He just meant we should forgive a lot, but His Jewish audience knew the number 77 appears only once in the Bible, in the story of Lamech, a vengeful man who returned offenses against him 77 times over (Genesis 4:23-24). Jesus was telling His followers to be as eager to forgive as Lamech was to seek revenge.

When you search for the Scripture Jesus hints at, you find that His teachings are more amazing than you first thought!

Now without faith it is impossible to please God, for whoever comes to him must believe that he exists and that he rewards those who diligently search for him.
Hebrews 11:6, ISV

THREE BIG WORDS

There's an ancient Jewish teaching from before the time of Jesus that says: "The world stands on three things: *Torah* (Scripture), *avodah* (worship), and *gimilut chasadim* (loving acts of kindness)."

To the Jews, these three pursuits were inseparable frameworks to building a relationship with God, each other, and the world. They were equal in importance.

What would happen if YOU gave equal time and emphasis to all three EVERY DAY?

I appeal to you therefore, brothers, by the mercies of God, to present your bodies as a living sacrifice, holy and acceptable to God, which is your spiritual worship.
Romans 12:1, *ESV*

WHAT'S IN A QUIET TIME?

I've always felt guilty about my morning "quiet time" because the idea of silent prayer, reading, and journaling has never inspired me. So I once asked a Jewish rabbi friend what he thought Jesus' "quiet time" might have looked like. He laughed at the idea of a "quiet time" because for centuries Jewish daily devotions have been anything but quiet! He told me that his daily devotion included public reading of Scripture, singing in worship, and praying loudly while walking and moving his whole body. It's anything but quiet, he told me.

So when Jesus did His "devotions," it's likely it would have looked less like sitting on the end of His bed with head bowed and eyes closed and more like a worship concert.

How will this idea change your "quiet time" today?

Shout joyfully to the LORD, all the earth.
Psalm 100:1

SHOUT JOYFULLY TO
LORD ALL THE EARTH

PSALM 100:1